CAROL ANN DUFFY was Poet Laureate of the
United Kingdom for a decade from 2009 to 2019.
Her poetry has received many awards, including
the Signal Prize for Children's Verse, the Whitbread,
Forward and T. S. Eliot Prizes, and the Lannan and
E. M. Forster Awards in America. She won the PEN
Pinter Prize in 2012, and was appointed DBE in 2015.
In 2021, she was awarded the International Golden
Wreath for lifetime achievement in poetry.

POLITICS

Carol Ann Duffy

PICADOR

First published 2023 by Picador
an imprint of Pan Macmillan
The Smithson, 6 Briset Street, London EC1M 5NR
EU representative: Macmillan Publishers Ireland Ltd, 1st Floor,
The Liffey Trust Centre, 117–126 Sheriff Street Upper,
Dublin 1, D01 YC43
Associated companies throughout the world
www.panmacmillan.com

ISBN 978-1-5290-9691-0

1 3 5 7 9 8 6 4 2

A CIP catalogue record for this book is available from the British Library.

Printed and bound by CPI Group (UK) Ltd, Croydon, CR0 4YY

MIX
Paper | Supporting
responsible forestry
FSC® C116313
www.fsc.org

Visit *www.picador.com* to read more about all our books
and to buy them. You will also find features, author interviews and
news of any author events, and you can sign up for e-newsletters
so that you're always first to hear about our new releases.

Contents

Education for Leisure

Today I am going to kill something. Anything.
I have had enough of being ignored and today
I am going to play God. It is an ordinary day,
a sort of grey with boredom stirring in the streets.

I squash a fly against the window with my thumb.
We did that at school. Shakespeare. It was in
another language and now the fly is in another language.
I breathe out talent on the glass to write my name.

I am a genius. I could be anything at all, with half
the chance. But today I am going to change the world.
Something's world. The cat avoids me. The cat
knows I am a genius and has hidden itself.

I pour the goldfish down the bog. I pull the chain.
I see that it is good. The budgie is panicking.
Once a fortnight, I walk the two miles into town
for signing on. They don't appreciate my autograph.

There is nothing left to kill. I dial the radio
and tell the man he's talking to a superstar.
He cuts me off. I get our bread-knife and go out.
The pavements glitter suddenly. I touch your arm.

1985

Debt

He was all night sleepless over money.
Impossible scenarios danced in the dark
as though he was drunk. The woman
stirred, a soft spoon, and what had emerged
from them dreamed in the next room, safe.
He left himself and drew a gun he didn't own.

He won the pools; pearls for her and ponies
for the kids. The damp bedroom was an ocean liner
till the woman farted, drifted on, away from him.
Despair formed a useless prayer and worry an ulcer.
He bargained with something he could not believe in
for something he could not have. *Sir* . . .

Through the wallpaper men in suits appeared.
They wanted the video, wanted the furniture.
They wanted the children. Sweat soured in nylon sheets
as his heartbeat panicked, trying to get out.
There was nothing he would not do. There was
nothing to do but run the mind's mad films.

Dear Sir . . . his ghost typed on. He remembered
waiting for her, years ago, on pay-day
with a bar of fruit-and-nut. Somehow consoled
he reached out, found her, and then slept.
Add this. Take that away. The long night leaked
cold light into the house. A letter came.

1985

The B Movie

At a preview of That Hagen Story *in 1947, when actor*
Ronald Reagan became the first person on screen to say 'I love
you, will you marry me?' to the nineteen-year-old Shirley
Temple, there was such a cry of 'Oh, no!' from the invited
audience that the scene was cut out when the film was released.

Lap dissolve. You make a man speak crap dialogue,
one day he'll make you eat your words. OK?
Let's go for a take. Where's the rest of me? *'Oh, no!'*

Things are different now. He's got star billing,
star wars, applause. Takes her in his arms.
I'm talking about a *real* weepie. Freeze frame. *'Oh, no!'*

On his say-so, the train wipes out the heroine
and there ain't no final reel. How do you like that?
My fellow Americans, we got five minutes. *'Oh, no!'*

Classic. He holds the onion to water such sorrow.
We need a Kleenex the size of Russia here, no kidding.
Have that kid's tail any time he wants to. *Yup.*

1985

Standing Female Nude

Six hours like this for a few francs.
Belly nipple arse in the window light,
he drains the colour from me. Further to the right,
Madame. And do try to be still.
I shall be represented analytically and hung
in great museums. The bourgeoisie will coo
at such an image of a river-whore. They call it Art.

Maybe. He is concerned with volume, space.
I with the next meal. You're getting thin,
Madame, this is not good. My breasts hang
slightly low, the studio is cold. In the tea-leaves
I can see the Queen of England gazing
on my shape. Magnificent, she murmurs
moving on. It makes me laugh. His name

is Georges. They tell me he's a genius.
There are times he does not concentrate
and stiffens for my warmth.
He possesses me on canvas as he dips the brush
repeatedly into the paint. Little man,
you've not the money for the arts I sell.
Both poor, we make our living how we can.

I ask him Why do you do this? Because
I have to. There's no choice. Don't talk.
My smile confuses him. These artists
take themselves too seriously. At night I fill myself
with wine and dance around the bars. When it's finished
he shows me proudly, lights a cigarette. I say
Twelve francs and get my shawl. It does not look like me.

1985

Politico

Corner of Thistle Street, two slack shillings jangled
in his pocket. Wee Frank. Politico. A word in the right ear
got things moving. *A free beer for they dockers
and the guns will come through in the morning. Nae bother.*

Bread rolls and Heavy came up the rope to the window
where he and McShane were making a stand. *Someone
sent up a megaphone, for Christ's sake.* Occupation.
Aye. And the soldiers below just biding their time.

Blacklisted. Bar L. *That scunner, Churchill.* The Clyde
where men cheered theirselves out of work as champagne
butted a new ship. Spikes at the back of the toilet seat.
Alls I'm doing is fighting for wur dignity. Away.

*Smoke-filled rooms? Wait till I tell you . . . Listen,
I'm ten years dead and turning in my urn. Socialism?
These days?* There's the tree that never grew. *Och,
a shower of shites.* There's the bird that never flew.

1987

8

Foreign

Imagine living in a strange, dark city for twenty years.
There are some dismal dwellings on the east side
and one of them is yours. On the landing, you hear
your foreign accent echo down the stairs. You think
in a language of your own and talk in theirs.

Then you are writing home. The voice in your head
recites the letter in a local dialect; behind that
is the sound of your mother singing to you,
all that time ago, and now you do not know
why your eyes are watering and what's the word for this.

You use the public transport. Work. Sleep. Imagine one
    night
you saw a name for yourself sprayed in red
against a brick wall. A hate name. Red like blood.
It is snowing on the streets, under the neon lights,
as if this place were coming to bits before your eyes.

And in the delicatessen, from time to time, the coins
in your palm will not translate. Inarticulate,
because this is not home, you point at fruit. Imagine
that one of you says *Me not know what these people mean.
It like they only go to bed and dream.* Imagine that.

1987

Yes, Officer

It was about the time of day you mention, yes.
I remember noticing the quality of light
beyond the bridge. I lit a cigarette.

I saw some birds. I knew the words for them
and their collective noun. A skein of geese. This cell
is further away from anywhere I've ever been. Perhaps.

I was in love. *For God's sake, don't.*
Fear is the first taste of blood in a dry mouth.
I have no alibi. Yes, I used to have a beard.

No, no. I wouldn't use that phrase. The more you ask
the less I have to say. There was a woman crying
on the towpath, dressed in grey. *Please*. Sir.

Without my own language, I am a blind man
in the wrong house. Here come the fists, the boots.
I curl in a corner, uttering empty vowels until

they have their truth. That is my full name.
With my good arm I sign a forgery. Yes, Officer,
I did. I did and these, your words, admit it.

1987

11

Deportation

They have not been kind here. Now I must leave,
the words I've learned for supplication,
gratitude, will go unused. Love is a look
in the eyes in any language, but not here,
not this year. They have not been welcoming.

I used to think the world was where we lived
in space, one country shining in big dark.
I saw a photograph when I was small.

Now I am *Alien*. Where I come from there are few jobs,
the young are sullen and do not dream. My lover
bears our child and I was to work here, find
a home. In twenty years we would say This is you
when you were a baby, when the plum tree was a shoot . . .

We will tire each other out, making our homes
in one another's arms. We are not strong enough.

They are polite, recite official jargon endlessly.
Form F. Room 12. Box 6. I have felt less small
below mountains disappearing into cloud
than entering the Building of Exile. Hearse taxis
crawl the drizzling streets towards the terminal.

I am no one special. An ocean parts me from my love.

Go back. She will embrace me, ask what it was like.
Return. One thing – there was a space to write
the colour of her eyes. They have an apple here,
a bitter-sweet, which matches them exactly. Dearest,
without you I am nowhere. It was cold.

1987

Weasel Words

*It was explained to Sir Robert Armstrong that
'weasel words' are 'words empty of meaning, like an egg
which has had its contents sucked out by a weasel'.*

Let me repeat that we Weasels mean no harm.
You may have read that we are vicious hunters,
but this is absolutely not the case. Pure bias
on the part of your Natural History Book. *Hear, hear.*

We are long, slim-bodied carnivores with exceptionally
short legs and we have never denied this.
Furthermore, anyone here today could put a Weasel
down his trouser-leg and nothing would happen.
   Weasel laughter.

Which is more than can be said for the Ferrets opposite.
You can trust a Weasel, let me continue, a Weasel
does not break the spinal cord of its victim with one bite.
Weasel cheers. Our brown fur coats turn white in winter.

And as for eggs, here is a whole egg. It looks like an egg.
It is an egg. *Slurp*. An egg. *Slurp*. A whole egg.

Slurp . . . Slurp . . .

1990

Poet for Our Times

I write the headlines for a Daily Paper.
It's just a knack one's born with all-right-Squire.
You do not have to be an educator,
just bang the words down like they're screaming *Fire!*
CECIL-KEAYS ROW SHOCK TELLS EYETIE
    WAITER.
ENGLAND FAN CALLS WHINGEING FROG
    A LIAR.

Cheers. Thing is, you've got to grab attention
with just one phrase as punters rush on by.
I've made mistakes too numerous to mention,
so now we print the buggers inches high.
TOP MP PANTIE ROMP INCREASES TENSION.
RENT BOY: ROCK STAR PAID ME WELL TO
    LIE.

I like to think that I'm a sort of poet
for our times. My shout. Know what I mean?
I've got a special talent and I show it
in punchy haikus featuring the Queen.
DIPLOMAT IN BED WITH SERBO-CROAT.
EASTENDERS' BONKING SHOCK IS WELL-
    OBSCENE.

Of course, these days, there's not the sense of panic
you got a few years back. What with the box
et cet. I wish I'd been around when the Titanic
sank. To headline that, mate, would've been the tops.
SEE PAGE 3 TODAY GENTS THEY'RE
    GIGANTIC.
KINNOCK-BASHER MAGGIE PULLS OUT
    STOPS.

And, yes, I have a dream — make that a scotch, ta —
that kids will know my headlines off by heart.
IMMIGRANTS FLOOD IN CLAIMS HEATHROW
    WATCHER.
GREEN PARTY WOMAN IS A NIGHTCLUB
    TART.
The poems of the decade . . . *Stuff 'em! Gotcha!*
The instant tits and bottom line of art.

1990.

Making Money

Turnover. Profit. Readies. Cash. Loot. Dough. Income.
    Stash.
Dosh. Bread. Finance. Brass. I give my tongue over
to money; the taste of warm rust in a chipped mug
of tap-water. Drink some yourself. Consider
an Indian man in Delhi, Salaamat the *niyariwallah*,
who squats by an open drain for hours, sifting shit
for the price of a chapati. More than that. His hands
in crumbling gloves of crap pray at the drains
for the pearls in slime his grandfather swore he found.

Megabucks. Wages. Interest. Wealth. I sniff and snuffle
for a whiff of pelf; the stench of an abattoir blown
by a stale wind over the fields. Roll up a fiver,
snort. Meet Kim. Kim will give you the works,
her own worst enema, suck you, lick you, squeal
red weals to your whip, be nun, nurse, nanny,
nymph on a credit card. Don't worry.
Kim's only in it for the money. Lucre. Tin. Dibs.

I put my ear to brass lips; a small fire's whisper
close to a forest. Listen. His cellular telephone
rings in the Bull's car. Golden hello. Big deal. Now get
    this
straight. *Making a living is making a killing these days.*
Jobbers and brokers buzz. He paints out a landscape
by number. The Bull. Seriously rich. Nasty. One of us.

Salary. Boodle. Oof. Blunt. Shekels. Lolly. Gelt. Funds.
I wallow in coin, naked; the scary caress of a fake hand
on my flesh. Get stuck in. Bergama. The boys from the
    bazaar
hide on the target-range, watching the soldiers fire.
    Between bursts,
they rush for the spent shells, cart them away for scrap.
Here is the catch. Some shells don't explode. Ahmat
runs over grass, lucky for six months, so far. So
bomb-collectors die young. But the money's good.

Palmgrease. Smackers. Greenbacks. Wads. I widen my
     eyes
at a fortune; a set of knives on black cloth, shining,
utterly beautiful. Weep. The economy booms
like cannon, far out at sea on a lone ship. We leave
our places of work, tired, in the shortening hours, in the
     time
of night our town could be anywhere, and some of us
     pause
in the square, where a clown makes money swallowing
     fire.

1990

Job Creation

for Ian McMillan

They have shipped Gulliver up north.
He lies at the edge of the town,
sleeping.
His snores are thunder in the night.

Round here, we reckon they have drugged him
or we dream he is a landscape
which might drag itself up and walk.

Here are ropes, they said.
Tie him down.
We will pay you.
Tie Gulliver down with these ropes.

I slaved all day at his left knee,
until the sun went down
behind it
and clouds gathered on his eyes

and darkness settled on his shoulders
like a job.

1990

22

Fraud

Firstly, I changed my name
to that of a youth I knew for sure had bought it in
    1940, Rotterdam.
Private M.
I was my own poem,
pseudonym,
rule of thumb.
What was my aim?
To change from a bum
to a billionaire. I spoke the English. Mine was a scam
involving pensions, papers, politicians in-and-out of
    their pram.
And I was to blame.

For what? There's a gnome
in Zürich knows more than people assume.
There's a military man, Jerusalem
way, keeping schtum.
Then there's Him –
for whom
I paid for a butch and femme
to make him come.

And all of the crème
de la crème
considered me scum.

Poverty's dumb.
Take it from me, Sonny Jim,
learn to lie in the mother-tongue of the motherfucker
    you want to charm.
They're all the same,
turning their wide blind eyes to crime.
And who gives a damn
when the keys to a second home
are pressed in his palm,
or polaroids of a Night of Shame
with a Boy on the Game
are passed his way at the A.G.M.?

So read my lips. Mo-ney. Pow-er. Fame.
And had I been asked, in my time,
in my puce and prosperous prime,
if I recalled the crumbling slum
of my Daddy's home,
if I was a shit, a sham,
if I'd done immeasurable harm,
I could have replied with a dream:

the water that night was calm
and with my enormous mouth, in bubbles and blood
   and phlegm,
I gargled my name.

1993

Mrs Faust

First things first –
I married Faust.
We met as students,
shacked up, split up,
made up, hitched up,
got a mortgage on a house,
flourished academically,
BA. MA. Ph.D. No kids.
Two towelled bathrobes. Hers. His.

We worked. We saved.
We moved again.
Fast cars. A boat with sails.
A second home in Wales.
The latest toys – computers,
mobile phones. Prospered.
Moved again. Faust's face
was clever, greedy, slightly mad.
I was as bad.

I grew to love the lifestyle,
not the life.
He grew to love the kudos,
not the wife.
He went to whores.
I felt, not jealousy,
but chronic irritation.
I went to yoga, t'ai chi,
Feng Shui, therapy, colonic irrigation.

And Faust would boast
at dinner parties
of the cost
of doing deals out East.
Then take his lust
to Soho in a cab,
to say the least,
to lay the ghost,
get lost, meet panthers, feast.

He wanted more.
I came home late one winter's evening,
hadn't eaten.
Faust was upstairs in his study,
in a meeting.
I smelled cigar smoke,
hellish, oddly sexy, not allowed.
I heard Faust and the other
laugh aloud.

Next thing, the world,
as Faust said,
spread its legs.
First politics —
Safe seat. MP. Right Hon. KG.
Then banks —
offshore, abroad —
and business —
Vice-chairman. Chairman. Owner. Lord.

Enough? *Encore!*
Faust was Cardinal, Pope,
knew more than God;
flew faster than the speed of sound
around the globe,
lunched;
walked on the moon,
golfed, holed in one;
lit a fat Havana on the sun.

Then backed a hunch –
invested in smart bombs,
in harms,
Faust dealt in arms.
Faust got in deep, got out.
Bought farms,
cloned sheep,
Faust surfed the Internet
for like-minded Bo-Peep.

As for me,
I went my own sweet way,
saw Rome in a day,
spun gold from hay,
had a facelift,
had my breasts enlarged,
my buttocks tightened;
went to China, Thailand, Africa,
returned, enlightened.

Turned 40, celibate,
teetotal, vegan,
Buddhist, 41.
Went blonde,
redhead, brunette,
went native, ape,
berserk, bananas;
went on the run, alone;
went home.

Faust was in. *A word,* he said,
I spent the night being pleasured
by a virtual Helen of Troy.
Face that launched a thousand ships.
I kissed its lips.
Thing is —
I've made a pact
with Mephistopheles,
the Devil's boy.

He's on his way
to take away
what's owed,
reap what I sowed.
For all these years of
gagging for it,
going for it,
rolling in it,
I've sold my soul.

At this, I heard
a serpent's hiss,
tasted evil, knew its smell,
as scaly devil hands
poked up
right through the terracotta Tuscan tiles
at Faust's bare feet
and dragged him, oddly smirking, there and then
straight down to Hell.

Oh, well.
Faust's will
left everything –
the yacht,
the several homes,
the Lear jet, the helipad,
the loot, et cet, et cet,
the lot –
to me.

C'est la vie.
When I got ill,
it hurt like hell.
I bought a kidney
with my credit card,
then I got well.
I keep Faust's secret still —
the clever, cunning, callous bastard
didn't have a soul to sell.

1999

Loud

Parents with mutilated children have been turned away from the empty hospital and told to hire smugglers to take them across the border to Quetta, a Pakistani frontier city at least six hours away by car.

(Afghanistan, 28 October 2001)

The News had often made her shout,
but one day her voice ripped out of her throat
like a firework, with a terrible sulphurous crack
that made her jump, a flash of light in the dark.
Now she was loud.

Before, she'd been easily led,
one of the crowd, joined in with the national whoop
for the winning goal, the boos for the bent MP, the cheer
for the royal kiss on the balcony. Not any more. Now
she could roar.

She practised alone at home, found
she could call abroad without using the phone, could sing
like an orchestra in the bath, could yawn like thunder
watching TV. She switched to the News. It was all about
Muslims, Christians, Jews.

Then her scream was a huge bird
that flew her away into the dark; each vast wing a shriek,
awful to hear, the beak the sickening hiss of a thrown spear.
She stayed up there all night, in the wind and rain, wailing,
uttering lightning.

Down, she was pure sound, rumbling
like an avalanche. She bit radios, swallowed them, gargled
their News, till the words were – *ran into the church and
  sprayed*
the congregation with bullets no one has claimed – gibberish,
  crap,
in the cave of her mouth.

Her voice stomped through the city,
shouting the odds, shaking the bells awake in their towers.
She yelled through the countryside, swelling the rivers,
    felling
the woods. She put out to sea, screeching and bellowing,
spewing brine.

She bawled at the moon and it span away
into space. She hollered into the dark where fighter planes
buzzed at her face. She howled till every noise in the world
sang in the spit on the tip of her tongue: the shriek of a
    bomb,
the bang of a gun,

the prayers of the priest, the pad of the feet
in the mosque, the casual rip of the post, the mothers' sobs,
the thump of the drop, the President's cough, the screams
of the children cowering under their pews, loud, loud,
louder, the News.

2002

Politics

How it makes your face a stone
that aches to weep, your heart a fist,
clenched or thumping, your tongue
an iron latch with no door; your right hand
a gauntlet, a glove-puppet the left, your laugh
a dry leaf twitching in the wind, your desert island discs
hiss hiss hiss, the words on your lips dice
that throw no six.
              How it takes the breath
away, the piss, your kiss a dropped pound coin,
your promises latin, feedback, static, gibberish,
your hair a wig, your gait a plankwalk. How it says
politics – to your education, fairness, health; shouts
Politics! – to your industry, investment, wealth; roars,
    to your
conscience, moral compass, truth, *POLITICS*
    POLITICS.

2011

Big Ask

What was it Sisyphus pushed up the hill?
I wouldn't call it a rock.
Will you solemnly swear on the Bible?
I couldn't swear on a book.
With which piece did you capture the castle?
I shouldn't hazard a rook.

When did the President give you the date?
Nothing to do with Barack!
Were 1200 targets marked on a chart?
Nothing was circled in black.
On what was the prisoner stripped and stretched?
Nothing resembling a rack.

Guantanamo Bay – how many detained?
How many grains in a sack?
Extraordinary Rendition – give me some names.
How many cards in a pack?
Sexing the Dossier – name of the game?
Poker. Gin Rummy. Blackjack.

Who planned the deployment of shock and awe?
I didn't back the attack.
Inside the Mosque, please describe what you saw.
I couldn't see through the smoke.
Your estimate of the cost of the War?
I had no brief to keep track.

Where was Saddam when they found him at last?
Maybe holed under a shack.
What happened to him once they'd kicked his ass?
Maybe he swung from the neck.
The WMD . . . you found the stash?
Well, maybe not in Iraq.

2011

September 2014

Tha gaol agam ort

A thistle can draw blood,
                              so can a rose,
growing together
where the river flows, shared currency
across a border it can never know;
where, somewhen, Rabbie Burns might swim
or pilgrim Keats come walking
out of love for him.
                              Aye, here's to you,
cousins, sisters, brothers,
in your brave, bold, brilliant land.
The thistle jags our hearts —
take these roses
                              from our bloodied hands.

2014

Campaign

In which her body was a question-mark
querying her lies; her mouth a ballot-box that bit
the hand that fed. Her eyes? They swivelled for a
jackpot win. Her heart was a stolen purse;
her rhetoric an empty vicarage, the windows smashed.
Then her feet grew sharp stilettos, awkward.
Then she had balls, believe it. When she woke,
her nose was bloody, difficult. The furious young
ran towards her through the fields of wheat.

2017

Anonymous

The King didn't sign, but a scribe
with a fair hand wrote it all down
and the King thought the men in the meadow
dogs, for taking the shine off the crown;
afterwards fumed, fitted, foamed
at the mouth. Those from the North
rode north, not believing a word
they'd heard from the weasel King,
who'd tax the fart from your arse,
razored their falchions.

Nice meadow, Runnymede; where an English oak
made a mirror of shade, next to the Thames,
where a knight could kick off his boots
to paddle in clover. A horse lifting its tail
to crap. A bishop pissing into the river.
The King like a chesspiece, wooden, white.
A pawn of a page from the distant castle.
Widows and nuns took up their threads,
wove the scene into tapestry – but not
those mongrels rutting under the tree.

Green and gold for the smock of the pretty page;
rust for his hair. His face pink as the peach
he passed to the King on a pewter plate –
his life nothing to no one, then or now, except
he was there, like the swans, the dragonflies,
the wasp circling the sucked, chucked pit of a drupe.
Weft and warp – for here comes the bit
where the boss baron stands to intone
the grave nuances of the grievances . . .
Quod Anglicana ecclesia libera sit . . .

Now, I was a luckless loutess of a troubadour,
offstage, as it were, mending my lute
on the riverbank – I kenned not then
that my posthumous fame would rest in *Anonymous* –
and I earwigged in as those wadded counts
laid it down to the King. *And another thing . . .
and another thing . . .* The field had filled
with tents, servants, banners, mounts,
and, being the girl of a villein who'd died unfree,
I reckoned this business had nowt to do with me . . .

Earls and Barons are not to be amerced
save by their peers . . . though I tuned my ears
at *Una mensura vini through all our Kingdom*
and one measure of ale. I'd been on the road
for a year and a bard likes to guarantee
the size of her beer. But when I heard
To no one will we sell, to no one
will we deny or delay, right or justice,
I thought Too Bloody Right. I strummed in key.
The words sharpened the air, like liberty.

2018

In The Drowned Bookshop

Inhoop, Inhospitable, Inhospitality,
Inhuman: lacking kindness, pity or compassion;
cruel, indifferent – a dictionary drifts, open at I.
I beg to differ.

        An A to Z of Mammals, spoiled,
sinks. Not human, the beached whales of Skegness.
Nor the river, skimmed though it has each poem,
biography, Once Upon A Time . . .

                Poor tomes;
nothing to be learned from them by the human inhuman.
In splashes the tardy Minister for Floods, smart
despite cheap new wellingtons, austere.
There bobs *Mary I of England, 1516–1558*;
Calais written on her heart.

2018

45

The Ex-Ministers

They rise above us, the ex-ministers,
in private jets, left wing, right wing, drop low
to Beijing, Kuwait, the Congo, Kazakhstan;
their deals and contracts in the old red boxes,
for sentimental reasons.

Beyond our shores,
they float on superyachts, *Nostrovia!*,
guests of the mortal gods; the vague moon a bitcoin.
We are nothing to them now; lemmings
going over the white cliffs of Dover.

And when they are here, they are unseen;
chauffeured in blacked-out cars to the bars
in the heavens – far, glittering shards –
to look down
on our lucrative democracy.

Though they have bought the same face,
so they will know each other.

2018

46

Britannia

A day fifty years ago surfaces
as I watch the rolling news
in the days after Grenfell
and somebody screams *Bastards!* off-camera.

We had been asked to bring
a sixpence, a shilling, a florin,
when they held the special assembly
for Aberfan.

       My father shouted
the Coal Board were *criminals, murderers*;
raged again when they looted the Fund.
I should not connect the two, but I do:

the school drowned in slurry
on the small black-and-white screen;
the tower in flames on full-colour plasma.
The constant, dutiful Queen.

2018

Gorilla

It was at Berlin Zoo – don't ask –
where I came face to thick glass
with a gorilla.

              We stared each other out.
Its eyes were smashed rage
under a pelmet of wrath.
Its nose, two boxing-gloves.
Its mouth, an unliftable curse; I wished
it were free,

              down on the equatorial belt,
chilling to Morrissey.
With a day's more evolution, it could even be President.

2018

Swearing In

Combover, thatch-fraud, rug-rogue, laquer-lout;
twitter-rat, tweet-twat, tripe-gob, muckspout.

Sleaze-serf, poke-knave, bribe-berk, bedswerver;
hand-mangler, kids-mitts, thumb-sucker, fist-jerker.

News-maggot, lie-monger, tongue-trickster, crap-grubber;
smell-feast, guzzle-chops, snout-ligger, burger-blubber.

Tie-treader, tan-faker, draft-dodger, piss-douse;
fraud-hawker, golf-plonker, bigot-merchant, shite-louse.

Mandrake Mymmerkin, welcome to the White House.

2018

A Formal Complaint

Where do they keep coming from, these arseholes
who, when we were young, were the gatekeepers?
They must have been young then too, the chancers
who smirk and sidle and spin; the tossers
who blag and bray and brag; the bullshitters
who pose and pontificate; the patriots.

They do not mean us well, these patriots,
with their buttock-faced smarm, the pursed arseholes
of their non-disclosures – perfect for bullshitting.
Though we demonstrate at the gate, keepers
of small flames, it is bollocks they toss us
over the railings, airwaves; taking their chances.

For they love a good gamble, these chancers;
all suited and booted as patriots,
or kilted to clap the caber-tossers
over the border; midgies biting their arseholes.
No latecomers among the gatekeepers –
they start early; interns for bullshitters.

Your remote-control is a bullshit
detector. Turn off the fat puce chancer

who has found No Evidence of gatekeepers
acting as anything but patriots.
He is talking out of his arse; whole
generations, communities, scrapped, tossed.

Because it's profit, not loss, for tossers.
Birthsigns compatible with bullshitters,
they stick together – Uranus in arseholes –
under the lucky stars of the chancers.
What's your sign? It better be Patriot
or your future's void with the gatekeepers.

But now, it's Blessed are the Gatekeepers
who bar your progress like bouncers; tossers
out of non-members of Club Patriot.
And they're playing tonight, The Bullshitters.
And they rate themselves as dancers, chancers.
They want to wake up with an arsehole.

No. Give me a gatekeeper who smells bullshit;
with two rottweilers, Tosser and Chancer,
to leave of fake patriots only their arseholes.

2018

Sleeping Place (What He Said)

Over the railings, headstones.
When they padlock the gates, over I climb.
Getting late.

Mourned, otherly cold, just bones,
it is only their names and dates they claim.
Signed-off mates.

What happens is, is they dig
the day before. The grey angels by night,
stunned, bereaved.

She squeezes through, my thin dog.
I follow her bark, like imagined light,
to a grave.

There's always a shallow one,
scooped out above grandparents, husbands, wives,
to be close.

So I've blagged this cheap red wine,
cane it; my spine to a pillar of lives,
still missed most.

I roll out the sleeping-bag
then crawl in with the dog on top; half-pissed,
sick, coughing.

You see their hands when you beg;
a handful of coins; a handful of dust
on a coffin.

2018

The Wound In Time

It is the wound in Time. The century's tides,
chanting their bitter psalms, cannot heal it.
Not the war to end all wars; death's birthing place;
the earth nursing its ticking metal eggs, hatching
new carnage. But how could you know, brave
as belief as you boarded the boats, singing?
The end of God in the poisonous, shrapneled air.
Poetry gargling its own blood. We sense it was love
you gave your world for; the town squares silent,
awaiting their cenotaphs. What happened next?
War. And after that? War. And now? War. War.
History might as well be water, chastising this shore,
for we learn nothing from your endless sacrifice.
Your faces drowning in the pages of the sea.

2018

Peterloo

Take down in your mind the Midland Hotel,
brick by brick, until the suites and rooms,
the bars and restaurants, are only air.

Unthink the Bridgewater Hall; let the orchestra
pack up its instruments, depart as ghosts.
Look hard and swear the Town Hall is not there.

Vanish the Library. Absolve the Conference Centre
of its presence here; ditto the trams, the cars.
Now see an open field – St Peter's Field –

set back, the Church; down the eastern side,
a walled garden, terraced houses; to the north,
the Quaker Meeting Place; a burial ground.

And on the skyline, factory chimneys, black
but smokeless – it being Sunday – their sour breath
still rancid on the wheezy, summer breeze.

So this is then. Four jobsworths clear the field
of stones. Ten magistrates wipe greasy breakfasts
from their chops. Four hundred special constables line up.

The North-West's finest – not – the Yeomanry, fire up
their seething truculence with booze and brags.
Weekend soldiers – see – their swords are cold, shiny-keen.

And, slinking to the house of Law, the local spies
who sell their lies for cash. How can you suss
whose son or brother makes that kind of deal?

Here comes my voice; one of thousands on the roads
to Manchester, from Oldham, Royton, Crompton,
Rochdale, Lees and Saddleworth . . . as to a gala day.

Each town or village has its marching band,
and we keep order to the drums, the spoons and pots,
hold our banners, wedding-sheets, high up on poles;

so if you look down Deansgate at our human flood,
you'll read our words. *No Corn Laws. Universal Suffrage.*
Justice. Love. We will have Liberty . . .

Now, I have these moments of my life before, before . . .
though I do not know this; lifting the hem of my best
white frock clear of the sooty street, stepping

on to the field. *Rule, Britannia*, we sing, all one –
Bury and Bolton, Eccles, Irlam, Salford, Stalybridge,
Stretford, Stockport, Wigan. *God Save the King*, we sing.

Then my body part of the broth of the crowd;
children bobbed to the top on the shoulders of men;
pale faces poor as potato peel under the bright flags.

We sweat hope. Because we are many, we think
we count. We chant rough poetry, full of its daft power.
Not one of us senses that this is the wrong time, wrong

time. And now my feet are not on this earth
and if I could breathe I would only breathe in
the heart of the man whose chest is pressed

to my face; who dances me round and around
in a mass and a mess of flesh, till we fall
at the edge of the grass, under a rearing horse.

But I was at school with him, the drunk lout
who leers down from the saddle. *Thomas
Ogden! I was at school with you! I know your Mam.*

And he knows me. But why does this anger him;
calling me *Witch* as he slices the air
with his sword. *I'll reform you, bitch!* Merciless

conductor: the wild music of our screams, squeezed
from our lungs as we fall; slashed from our throats
as we run. Yeomanry. Cavalry. Infantry. Bayonets.

Horse-hooves. Steel. Blood on my dress. If I could live,
I would ask what difference they'll make, these minutes
widening to centuries. Or hear your future answering
    voice,

as the Conservative Party check into their rooms
at the Midland Hotel for their annual Conference,
under the fluttering *One Nation* flags.

2019